RIGHT

GLORY

Revealing Power Of God's Glory

Wale Oyeniyi

FOLLOW US ON FACEBOOK

1. <u>**Like our Page on Facebook**</u>, submit prayer requests and follow powerful daily prayers for total victory and breakthrough

This title and others are available for quantity discounts for sale promotions, gifts, and evangelism. Visit our website or email us to get started.

Dedication

This book is dedicated to the sovereign God, Jesus Christ and the Holy Ghost.

Acknowledgement

To God be all glory, honour and praise for His utmost grace upon my life for seeing through the birthing of this book after several postponements.

I wish to say a sincere thank you to Mrs Tope Ayodele who sacrificially edited the manuscript. Without her, the work would have been incomplete. Thank you dearly for your patience and sacrifice to deliver the book on schedule.

I commend Dcns. Yemi Adesote for her invaluable input to the work. I am indebted to the encouragement, inspiration and love received from numerous colleagues, sons and daughters in the Lord who made various contributions that helped me in the process of learning and applying God's principles that are shared in the book.

My lovely wife, Adeola, David, Blessing and Miracle are exceedingly appreciated. My world is empty without you. You are greatly treasured.

Contents

Introduction 8

Chapter One: God's Glory 12

   How God's Glory Can Be Acquired 26

Chapter Two: Transforming Story To Glory............. 39

   Criteria for transformation 41

   Examples of Transformed Lives 45

Chapter Three: From Glory To Glory....................... 66

   Steps Required For Moving From Glory To Glory.

  75

Chapter Four: The Pain of Lost Glory........................97

   Some biblical examples of those who lost their glory

   99

Chapter Five: Recovering Lost Glory.......................122

   How Do We Recover Lost Glory? 127

   Sustaining the Recovered Glory 133

Chapter Six: A Stone Shall Not Replace Me; Use Me Oh Lord..142

Why God Will Not Use You................................ 151

How Can I Make God Use Me? 153

Chapter Seven: Glory In Heaven..........................160

The Blessedness of Heaven................................162

Benefits of Making Heaven................................165

Conclusion 173

Other Books by the Same Author.......................177

About the Author..178

Introduction

GLORY REVEALED

When a slave becomes the master,

And a prisoner the Prime-minister,

When a follower becomes the leader,

A loser the winner,

And a victim the victor,

Then glory is revealed.

When the sick becomes healed,

And an applicant; the employer of labour

When the barren becomes a joyful mother of children,

And darkness turns to light

When ashes turn to beauty, mourning to dancing,

And captivity turn to freedom

Then glory is revealed

When the jungle turns to a city,

And a beggar lends to many nation,

When crying turns to laughter,

And rivers ceaselessly flow in the desert,

Then glory is revealed!

When an age-long desire is met,

When dry bones begin to shine anew

When rain falls on dry land and green grass sprouts,

And then a stunt becomes a baobab

And a desert to a forest,

Then glory is revealed!

When answers come to questions that hitherto defiled solutions,

When a ragged body glows under designers' apparel,

When a beggar lends to nations,

And the abandoned become celebrities,

Then glory is revealed.

When a once upon a time enemy of the gospel

Engage in aggressive evangelism

When bare-footed pedestrians become

chauffer driven in exotic cars

When the destitute become nation builders

And morons turn genius

Then glory is revealed!

When the Heaven opens,

And Christ appears in the cloud for all to see,

When the trumpet sounds,

That no ear can pretend not to receive the message,

When elect by GRACE shall be transformed,

And the dead in Him resurrects all for the

home-ward journey to REIGN in His

Kingdom,

Then glory will be revealed.

Will you allow God's glory to be revealed?
Our God reigns!

Chapter One: God's Glory

'.....all the earth shall be filled with the glory of the Lord' Numbers 14:21b

The word 'glory' usually creates an atmosphere of worship and evokes the presence of God. It is self dignifying and connotes great value. God is glorious and can confer glory on a man but no man can share the glory of God.

God's glory is the worship, praise and honour of Him. It is the external manifestation of His person. Another definition of glory is great beauty. In this context, 'great beauty' goes far beyond what the naked eye can behold. It stretches extensively to that which only the spiritual eye can visualize. The glory of God is in His beauty and His beauty is in His glory. This description may sound confusing but it actually expresses the magnificent existence of God and the efficacy of the power of His glory. We can therefore confidently conclude that God's glory encompasses both the internal and external manifestation of His person.

What comes to your mind when you think of the glory of God? His great works? His Excellency? His perfection? Or is it the revelation of Himself in Jesus Christ? Certainly, God's glory is displayed in these ways. But much more than these, the Bible describes the glory of God as the basis for all creation. Everything that exists has its existence in Him and for Him.

Romans 11:36 says,

"For of him, and through him, and to him, are all things: to whom be glory for ever, Amen."

The beauty of God is one of its kind and nothing compares with it. God Almighty Himself has ordained us (Christians) to be bearers of his glory. But how do we who are His image-bearers glorify Him? Do we fulfill our responsibility to glorify Him simply by being alive? No. We are called to glorify God actively and purposefully. He desires to see His glory revealed through us but this can be achieved only if we are ready and willing to do as He pleases. In Genesis 1:27-28, God clearly expresses and explains that we are bearers and carriers of His glory. His word as written in the Bible spelt it out that we were created in His image and likeness. God did not just create us because there was a need for us to fill the Earth; we were created for various purposes, all of which can be summarized to be for the purpose of glorifying His name. Of course, it is obvious that the creatures He made before the sixth day were not capable of manifesting His glory as man would. He needed something that represented His true image as a living God and the best option He had was man.

To further help us understand the nature and the essence of God's glory, we shall examine the following questions:

1. What was the sole reason for creating man?

2. How do you recognize God's glory in the life of a man?

3. How accessible is the glory of God?

4. Can an unbeliever carry God's glory?

5. Can you share God's glory with Him?

1. What was the sole reason for creating man?

Isaiah 43:21 says expressly, *"This people have I formed for myself; they shall shew forth my praise."* God created us to show forth His praise and make known His glory. No man is born for the sake of being born. We are all born with anointing for various reasons and diverse missions to fulfill the revelation of His great and unfading glory. Therefore, making good use of the gift He has deposited in us glorifies Him and that means that His glory is revealed through us.

In the book of 1 Timothy 4:14-15, we are enjoined not to neglect the gift that God has bestowed on us. This means the glory of God will be revealed through us and be visible to everybody, i.e. when His glory is shown through us. Many people today are opaque. This is what happens when Jesus is not in the life of a person. The light of God cannot pass through such a person and for that reason, the glory of God cannot be revealed through him. Also, a believer who claims to have given his live to Christ but still lives in sin has lost his transparency. The glory of God in man is expressive and explosive. It is radiant and active rather than dormant and quiet.

2. How do you recognize God's glory in the life of a man?

Anyone who carries the glory of God does great exploit even when so little is expected of him. Such a person's head is raised above his equal. He declares a rising when others lament, ways are made for him even in the wilderness, and paths are created for him across the sea. The Bible also confirms this in Isaiah 43:2.The glory of God attracts help. It attracts favour; bringing patronage and increasing sales.

When the glory of God is revealed or expressed through someone or through a situation or a thing, it is usually beyond normal human reasoning and comprehension. Sometime in the U.S.A., Scientists discovered a new specie of bee and they named it 'the Bumble Bee'. The ability of this bee was underrated and criticized. They said the bumble bee would never be able to fly because its body was larger than its wings and therefore it was tagged 'grounded forever'. They spoke from human reasoning and scientific laws (aerodynamics). However, when it was time for the glory of God to be revealed through the small creature, all scientific laws were suspended and divine laws took over. The bumble bee stood one day, shook its wings, and began to fly.

It was beyond the imagination of the scientists and the flight proved them wrong. If divine laws override scientific laws in animals, how much more in humans? When the Lord is ready to have His glory revealed through us, all natural laws are displaced and suspended so as to allow His word which says all things are possible to take over the situation.

Another scientific law which the divine law has proved wrong is that which says "What goes up must come down". The proponent of the law must have been ignorant of or purposely ignored the effect of the presence of the glory of God in man. When a child of God who pleases Him and loves Him unconditionally is lifted, nothing on earth can ever pull him down. When he is blessed, he cannot be cursed. The life and lifestyle of such a person always proves all natural laws wrong because the glory of God will cause His brightness to shine through and the beauty of God will be seen and felt through him. He will be respected, loved and accepted wherever he goes. Those who looked down on him in the past will begin to look up to him; those who hissed at him will kneel at his feet, and those who named him a failure will turn round to call him 'Master. '

3. How accessible is the glory of God?

The glory of God is always available to shine through us but this is not feasible except a sign of preparedness is shown. The glory never descends on a man who will not express it in the right way, at the right place and at the right time. The Bible explains in Romans 3:23 that the glory of God has been made available for us 'all'. It is worthy to note here that glory is accessible to all irrespective of gender, age or educational achievements but sin is a great factor that deprives us of the right to His uncontroversial glory. The deprivation can be converted to provision in excess supply when we confess and forsake our sins. A life that is still in sin is not an ideal dwelling place and therefore cannot accommodate the glory of God who is emblem of purity, an icon of sanctity and a paragon of holiness.

1 Corinthians 3:16-17 sheds more light on why we should live a sinless life. These verses declare that anyone who defiles the spirit of God shall be destroyed. Undoubtedly, a man who is destroyed loses the glory of God. In 1 Timothy 3:16, the Bible also speaks of the glory which God receives when a Christian lives a godly life. When a spiritually filthy person seeks the glory of God to   be revealed through him, it is as one seeking a bride dressed in her wedding gown to sleep in a sty. It sounds rather asinine than awkward. A man who lives holy belongs to the flock of God Almighty, who is the undisputable shepherd

and His glory promises eternal life for such a person(John 10:28).

4. Can an unbeliever carry God's glory?

Sometimes, we see situations whereby a person who has not fulfilled all righteousness carries the glory of God and we wonder if God has become inequitable.

The answer is "no". God can never be one-sided, unjust or discriminatory. He has a reason for everything He does, and a good one at that. The ungodly rise to the place of glory just to fall after a while. They are raised to be disgraced. A good example is king Nebuchadnezzar. He was made king not because he was the best candidate but because God had a reason for his rising. He was raised to fall and serve as deterrent to others. By virtue of arrogance, he lost the glory. You shall not lose the glory of God on you to pride, arrogance or any vice in Jesus' name. '

A Christian who loses the glory of God becomes rejected where he had previously been accepted. He becomes a slave where he was once a master, and a tail where he was once a head. The praise he had been receiving for the things which he did right is traded for criticism. His beauty, strength and ability are lost until he gets back on track and does the right thing to recover the lost glory. A man who loses his glory also loses the grace; hence disgrace.

5. Can you share God's glory with Him?

Isaiah 42:8 says, "I am the LORD: that is my name: and my glory will I not give to another, neither my praise to graven images"

Each and every time I work hard towards achieving something great, I commit it into the hands of God and dedicate its success to the glory of His name by saying this small and meaningful prayer which has always worked for me better and quicker than magic. I say, "God, I make the effort, but the glory of the fruit of my labor is yours in Jesus' name". This short prayer has always helped me in attributing all the praise and glory I get from the success of my effort to God.

When I address a congregation and I am clapped, I see the hands as being put together for God and not for me. Why do I do so?

The answer is as simple as learning how to eat. God says he will raise stones to praise Him if no man to gives Him the glory He deserves. This means the gift and talent, the knowledge and the wisdom God has put in you are not by your power neither are they because you are the best person to receive them but for no other special purpose than to return all glory to Him. The moment you begin to ascribe the glory to your effort and ability is the moment your downfall begins. Only God is worthy to receive all glory as it is written in Revelations 4:11; *"Thou art worthy, O Lord, to receive glory and honour and power for thou hast created all things and for thy pleasure they are and were created"*. Every man is created for various good purposes, therefore, any action that is not aimed at returning the glory to God amounts to sharing His glory with Him and this is contrary to His word.

How God's Glory Can Be Acquired

God's glory can be acquired via various means. We shall discuss this in detail in the remaining portion of this chapter.

1. By Confession

David understood this in the book of 1 Chronicles 29:11 where he declares, "Thine, O Lord, is the greatness, and the power, and the glory, and the victory, and the majesty: for all that is in the heaven and in the earth is thine: thine is the kingdom, O Lord, and thou art exalted as head above all." When a Christian confesses that unto God is all greatness, glory, honour, power, majesty and victory, it is a way of appreciating the beauty of His name and authority and He in return blesses such a person by making available His ever-shining glory to be revealed through him.

Confession leads to possession. What we confess, we possess. Confessing Christ is as good as confessing God and confessing God is equivalent to confessing His glory because God is present in His son, Jesus Christ who is also present in the Father. Romans 10:9 sheds more light on confessing the glory of God; *"That if thou shalt confess with thy mouth the Lord Jesus, and shalt believe in thine heart that God hath raised him from the dead, thou shalt be saved"*

Undoubtedly, a person who is saved by God carries His glory. Without being told, we know that anyone who does not carry the glory of God is far from being saved. Such a person runs from debt to debt from trouble to trouble, ill-health to ill-health, failure to failure, poverty to penury until he is completely destroyed

2. By faith

Confession comes with faith. A Christian cannot confess what he does not believe in. The book of Matthew 6:30, challenges Christians of little faith, those who do not believe in the magnificent greatness of God, those who doubt the ability. The verse says, " *Wherefore, if God so clothe the grass of the field, which today is and tomorrow is cast into the oven, shall he not much more clothe you, O ye of little faith?*" This verse assures us that the beauty of God shall be revealed in our lives if we have faith. God, who reveals His glory though the beauty of the grass of the field that lives today and tomorrow is of no substantial value will do even more in beautifying believers who are made in His image.

Many people today do not carry the glory of God because they are afraid of it. May I declare that fear is an act of low faith or no faith at all. A carrier of faith does not fear. Rather, he sees obstacles (which are meant to bring fear) as stepping stones to his next level. Mark 4:40 *"...Why are ye so fearful? How is it that ye have no faith?"* This explains a good reason to have faith and be fearless. A further clarification of how faith begets glory is in the book of 1 John 5:4, *"For whatsoever is born of God overcometh the world: and this is the victory that overcometh the world, even our faith"*.

One who overcomes the world overcomes sickness, sorrow, poverty, disappointment, shame, disgrace, backwardness, death, barrenness, unemployment, sins and every problem of life because the glory of God lives with him but a person of no faith encounters difficulties in overcoming the world. The Bible also tells us in Luke 1:37 *that "For with God nothing shall be impossible."* This comes with believing that it is so and believing is an act of faith.

Having God's glory revealed through us is more than possible, if we have a mustard-seed faith and we are committed to doing what is right. We will definitely have His beauty communicated through us. In Mark 9:23 the Lord urges us to have faith, *"Jesus said unto him, if thou canst believe, all things are possible to him that believeth"*. Yes, He is right. The revelation of the glory of God through a man is possible if he believes.

3. By Thanksgiving

In 1 Chronicles 29:13, we see David giving thanks and praise to the glorious name of God. This is another way of acquiring the glory of God. I am also aware of the great sacrifice associated with thanking God. I always choose to thank Him for what I have and even the ones I do not have rather than ask Him for what I desire. Whether or not we ask God for something, He already knows that we are in need of them even many years before the need arises. It is rare to find people asking God to let them wake the next day but they do wake up and thank Him for giving them the grace to be living witnesses of the light of the new day.

Thanking Him rekindles His love and grace to us. Thus, when we have His grace, we have His glory revealed.

4. Making covenant with God

This is another means of acquiring God's glory. It also hastens the revelation of God through His children. In Haggai 2:5-7, God spoke to His people, referring to the covenant He made with them when He brought them out of Egypt. Based on this covenant, He promised to shake the heavens, the earth, the sea, the dry land and all nations and finally, fill His house with His glory. Those who covenant with God and keep to the agreement can acquire His glory. The covenant with God is not that of blood but of the spirit unto righteousness; doing what pleases Him and keeping His commandments without defaulting.

To people who have not tasted the beauty of God, they seemingly see keeping His commandments as a big, difficult and hilarious task. For someone on the outside, it may seem so but for those who have tried it and enjoyed the sweetness of His glory, this is not their experience at all. We can see this in 1 John 5:3 which says, *"For this is the love of*

God, that we keep his commandments: and his commandments are not grievous." Such people enjoy the enormity of the glory of God in their homes, families, work place and all other areas of their lives.

5. Sowing and giving

The seed we sow and what we give goes a long way in having the glory of God revealed through us. The book of Philippians chapter 4 verse 17 reads *"Not because I desire a gift: but I desire fruit that may abound to your account"*. Obviously, the fruit that will be plentiful to our account when we give is receiving more and it is an indication of the glory of God. The Bible also makes us to know in Philippians 4:19 that the Lord is rich in glory and through Jesus he will supply our needs. In verse 20, it says, *"Now unto God and our Father be glory for ever and ever".* Verses 19 and 20 serve as a confirmation to verse 17 regarding what will become of us if we cultivate the habit of giving. Giving begets receiving. Almost everybody is knowledgeable of the saying "givers never lack" but they rarely put it into practice. In Luke 6:38, the Bible talks about the reward of givers. When the glory of God radiates givers, it is absent in spendthrifts

When we give in the right way, we pave the way for receiving in hundred folds or in more and even more. Whenever we give to the needy, we are indirectly giving unto God. The Bible says in Proverbs 19:17 that *"He that hath pity upon the poor lendeth unto the LORD; and that which he hath given will he pay him again."* We know that God, who has said we will lend to nations and not borrow, the One who command us in Romans 13:8 to *"owe no man nothing but to love one another...",* that same God will never owe any man. When you give to the poor, you are by extension lending to Him and He will definitely repay you. A similar thing happens when we give to men of God.

In Matthew25:35-40, Jesus talks about diverse forms of giving and describe the ultimate beneficiary as God. Thus, when we clothe the poor, we are covering God's nakedness because it is unto the Lord. When we visit prisoners, we are visiting God. Whenever we feed the hungry, we are feeding God and when we take in strangers, it is unto Him. Interestingly, God does not owe man rather He rewards at a measureless degree

The most profitable investment is giving. God's acclamation that we shall lend to nations is pregnant with meaning. First, it means that we shall have in abundance and have surplus to give others far and near. However, it does not necessarily mean that the government of another nation will come to us for financial assistance or aid but when we give for the spread of the gospel to missions and missionaries in other nations of the world, we are lending to nations. On another hand, let's will recall in the book of Genesis 25:23, when Rebecca was pregnant of a set of twins. The Lord mentioned that she was carrying two nations. Each of the children was referred to as a 'nation'. This means that whenever you lend to individuals, the poor, those in need, you are lending to nations.

6. By asking

The glory of God can as well be obtained by asking for it. No child will ask his father for bread and be given a stone, or a snake for fish.

The Bible in Matthew 7:7- 8 gives a good reason why we need to ask. Of course, even without asking, He already knows what we want and desire but asking Him is challenging Him to do even more than we ask. It is comforting for a Christian to ask for the glory of God to be revealed through him and through the works of his hands. God, who is able to do exceeding abundantly above all that we ask or think according to the power that works in us is always available to listen to the cry of His children whom He has created in His own image and likeness(Ephesians 3:20). In John 14:13-15, the Lord promises to do whatever we ask in His name but we must do His will; which is to keep His commandments.

God does not derive pleasure in seeing His children deficient of his glory. He created us and desires to have His exquisiteness expressed though us. Therefore, if we approach Him in faith and with a pure heart, His glory will be made available to us all the days of our lives. If a wealthy earthly father can detests the sight of his children in a tattered dress, how much more God Almighty our heavenly father who is wealthier than wealth and richer than riches? He will definitely do more. I pray that God will give us the grace to ask Him for the revelation of His glory through us in the right way. May His glory indeed shine through us in Jesus' name.

The glory of God is the most essential material in life. A life that lacks is devoid of progress, fortune, success, prosperity, joy, grace, health and many other good things. A boss appears like a Servant when the glory of God is not present in him whereas a Slave is as good as the Master if the glory is revealed through him.

Chapter Two: Transforming Story To Glory

There is no glory without a story but when the former appears, it erases the evidences and the pains of the latter leaving its existence only to imagination. For example, when the glory of Jabez appeared, he forgot all the pains and shame of his old self and when we read the story now we can only imagine how it was. God is without doubt a God of glory and He delights in his children experiencing it to the fullest. The Bible tells us in Jeremiah 29:11 that, *"For I know the thoughts that I think toward you, saith the LORD, thoughts of peace, and not of evil, to give you an expected end."* Also, in Deuteronomy 8:18, the scripture states that, *"...for it is he (God) that giveth thee power to get wealth..."* We do have a confirmation in His word that all good and perfect gifts come from above. Now we can see that it is the delight of God for us to live in glory.

Therefore, anyone not manifesting or experiencing the glory of God is living below God's standard for his life. To live below His standard means to live a life of stories rather than of glory.

We understand through the scriptures that the purpose the Son of God (Jesus) was manifested is that he might destroy the works of the devil. The works of the devil is embedded in his three fold agenda, according to John 10:10, "...to steal, and to kill, and to destroy". The activity of the devil in the life of any man is what makes up his story. However, when transformation takes place, the story comes to an end and the glory is revealed.

Transformation means a complete change in someone which makes his life better than it was before. It is always a visible change that attracts people around. Before a person's story can be transformed into glory, three important things must be take place.

Criteria for transformation

1. Divine Encounter

Before a life of story can be transformed to a glorious one, there must be a divine encounter. An avenue has to be created for the individual to place his request before his creator. The ability of individual to know his hour of visitation is vital. This is seen in the life of Abraham in Genesis 18:2, when he recognized the three men who visited him as Angels of the Lord. He warmly welcomed them and ministered unto them and this singular act brought about the long awaited promise of a child. But for the timely recognition of the angels by Abraham, he would have missed that ample opportunity.

2. A Strong Desire For Change

Again, the life to be transformed must show a strong desire for a change. This means there must be a zeal for turn-around. The individual must be fed-up with his current situation. Until he gets to a state of desperation, the desired transformation may not come. Take for instance, the case of the Israelites in the land of Egypt. In Exodus 1, the scriptures record that the Israelites were fruitful and increased abundantly in their land of captivity. The more they were afflicted, the more they multiplied. This could only mean they were enjoying servitude. But, it got to a time when they could no longer bear the burdens. In Exodus 2:23 and Exodus 6:5 they cried unto the Lord for help. Only then did their divine encounter come. Long as you keep silent about your situation, heaven will take it that you are still enjoying the state.

3. Eschew Murmuring.

A life that will be transformed must not murmur. To murmur means to complain about something or somebody but not openly. Prayer is the best weapon to employ when you need a transformation to glory. As long as a person continues to murmur, the desired change will never come. What is more? God frowns at the act. It always brings stagnation and can even lead to destruction. The bible says in 1 Corinthians 10:10 that, *"Neither murmur ye, as some of them also murmured, and were destroyed of the destroyer."* We will observe this in the life of the Israelites after their deliverance from Egypt. Each time they encountered a challenge in the wilderness, they murmured against Moses instead of turning to God for solution. No wonder, their journey of forty days turned to forty years. Instead of murmuring, go on your knees and ask God for a change.

In the remaining part of this chapter, we shall look at some characters who enjoyed divine transformation. As we go on, I encourage you to note the distinct inputs that provoked their transformation. I trust God that you will experience your own transformation too in Jesus name.

Examples of Transformed Lives

1. **Abraham-** Abraham's life was full of stories and promises. Even at the age of ninety-nine (99), the promised child was not forthcoming. Each time God appeared to him, He affirmed His word, YET NOTHING HAPPENED until Abraham got tired and became desperate to have a legitimate child. In Genesis 15:2, he asked God in frustration *"...Lord God, what wilt thou give me, seeing I go childless, and the steward of my house is this Eliezer of Damascus?"* From that day, God began to work on his behalf and this brought about the divine encounter in Genesis 18 where three Angels visited him. The manifestation of that promise came in Genesis 21:1-8 when Sarah, his wife conceived and

bore a son, at the time God had promised. Abraham's life was transformed into glory at the birth of Isaac. The promise of God became visible. He had a son to survive him. It was through Isaac that the promise of Abraham being the father of many nations was fulfilled. The scripture says in Genesis 15:6 that *"And he believed in the Lord; and he counted it to him for righteousness"*.

2. **Jacob**- Joseph was a supplanter, a deceiver and cunning man. In Genesis 25:29-34, he usurped his brother, Esau. The undiscerning Esau fell for his ploy. Jacob also succeeded in taking Esau's blessings through the help of their mother, Rebecca. Jacob was labeled a deceiver of their millennium. After Esau's blessings, he

fled from home and became a wanderer. His story, however, was transformed when God stepped into his life in Genesis 28:13-14 *"13And behold, the Lord stood above it, and said, I am the Lord God of Abraham thy father, and the God of Isaac. The land whereon thou liest, to thee will I give it, and to thy seed; 14And thy seed shall be as the dust of the earth, and thou shalt spread abroad to the west, and to the east, and to the north and to the south: and in thee and in thy seed shall all the families of the earth be blessed"*. From that time on, Jacob became a man of glory.

It was in Jacob that God's promise to Abraham of being the father of many nations manifested. He became the father of the twelve tribes of Israel.

His name was changed by God from Jacob to Israel in Genesis 35:9-11 "*₉And God appeared unto Jacob again, when he came out of Padanaram, and blessed him.₁₀And God said unto him, Thy name is Jacob: thy name shall not be called anymore Jacob, but Israel shall be thy name: and he called his name Israel. ₁₁And God said unto him, I am God Almighty: be fruitful and multiply; a nation and a company of nations shall be of thee, and Kings shall come out of thy loins;*" God established Jacob and his story was transformed to glory.

3. **Jabez** - The mother of Jabez named him 'sorrow' and failure trailed him until he denounced the name. We understood the significance and

implications of names as the case may be. Little wonder then that God changed Abram's name to Abraham, Sarai to Sarah, Jacob to Israel, etc. so that His purpose for their lives could manifest.

Jabez became desperate for a change. In 1Chronicles 4:9-10, in verse 10, we read that *"And Jabez called on the God of Israel, saying, Oh that thou wouldest bless me indeed, and enlarge my coast, and that thine hand might be with me, and that thou wouldest keep me from evil, that it may not grieve me!...".* The Bible records that God granted him that which he requested.

4. **Ruth** – Ruth is a loyal lady was another person in the scripture whose

story was transformed to glory. She was a daughter of Moab. She married Mahon, the first son of Naomi the Bethlehemite. She became a widow at a very young age. When Naomi resolved to return to her home country after the death of her two sons and husband, Ruth cleaved to her. Orphar retreat did not dissuade her. Even her mother's-in-law entreaty did not make her bulge. She declared to the old woman 'intreat me not' to leave the' However, her story changed when she got married to Boaz, a wealthy man. That was not the end, Ruth, who was childless due to the early death of her first husband, conceived and bore a son named Obed. Obed became the grandfather of King David, the lineage through which our Lord Jesus Christ was born. Who could have imagined that a person whose life was filled with gloom would turn out to be a fore parent of Jesus the light of the whole world. That is the power of transformation.

5. **Hannah** - Hannah was the first of the two wives of her husband, Elkanah. She and her family had been going to Shiloh year after year as recorded in 1Samuel1:3 *"And this man went up out of his city yearly to worship and to sacrifice unto the lord of hosts in Shiloh..."* In verse 5, we read that," And her adversary also provoked her sore, for to make her fret because the Lord had shut up her womb."

Her journey to transformation began when she got frustrated because of her adversary's provocation. You will notice in verse 7 that the bible records that *"And as he did so year by year, when she went up to the Lord, so she provoked her, therefore she wept and did not eat"*. One particular year, she became desperate for a change and determined to wrestle with the Lord. In verses 10-11, *"And she was in bitterness of soul, and prayed unto the LORD, and wept sore. And she vowed a vow, and said, O LORD of hosts, if thou wilt indeed look on the affliction of thine hand maid, and remember me, and not forget thine handmaid, but wilt give unto thine handmaid a man child, then I will give him unto the LORD all the days of his life and there shall no razor come upon his head"* The result of this request was Samuel. Hannah's story was transformed to glory. She later had more children and had her name erased from the book of barrenness.

6. Mephibosheth - Mephibosheth was the only surviving grandson of King Saul. He was lame and thereafter abandoned. He was not living up to the standard of a prince that he was. He even proclaimed this in his word in 2 Samuel 9:8 *"And he bowed himself, and said, What is thy servant, that thou shouldest look upon such a dead dog as I am?"*

His story changed when there was a divine remembrance of him. In

1Samuel 20:15-16, David and Jonathan had made a covenant that David should not cut off his kindness from Jonathan's house for ever. But the covenant was not in force for Mephibosheth until 2 Samuel 9:1 when King David remembered it and asked if there was yet anyone left in the house of Saul to be compensated. Imagine what would have become of the crippled young man if David never remembered the covenant. His, situation would have remained the same.

When the name of Mephibosheth was mentioned, the King sent for him. That was the day he came into glory as all the land belonging to his grandfather was restored to him. He began to feast with the King and was brought into limelight (2Sam.9:10-11). Even as a lame man, he had many servants at his beck and call.

7. **Matthew**- Matthew was a Publican before he met the Lord Jesus Christ. Publicans in that era were charged with the collection of taxes and tributes. Many people hated them because they were usually Jew, collecting taxes for Rome. Moreover, they usually collected above the official charge. The payers were burdened while they fed fat as extortionist because of the relationship of the publicans with Rome, who are Gentiles. They regarded the publicans in the same category with prostitutes. This was the scenario Matthew found himself. He worked as a tax collector for a living

and was a reproach in the eyes of people around him.

There was however a transformation to glory for Matthew when the Lord passed his way and called him to be His disciple. The Bible records that Matthew left his post and followed Christ immediately. He, who people do not want to be identified with before then, became the Lord's disciple and was given the power to heal. He was with the Lord till his death. What a great privilege. What's more? He wrote the first book in the New Testament

8. **Peter:** Peter the Apostle was the first disciple called by our Lord Jesus Christ. He was a failure in his chosen fishing business. In Luke 5:5, The

Bible records that Peter had toiled all night and caught nothing. He was already washing his nets, which meant he was tired of toiling without results. He couldn't take it anymore. It was at that point that his divine encounter came. The Lord stepped into his boat and his story changed. His fame definitely spread a long way that day as the Lord took him from zero catch to a boat-sinking catch. From that day, he became a fisher of men. He became one of Jesus closest associates. He was with Him on the mountain of transfiguration and Gethsemane. He was so spirit filled that he discerned that Jesus is the son of God. God wrought so many signs and wonders by his hands so much that his shadows healed the sick. Acts 5:12-16.

9. The Demoniac of Gadarene - This was a man who was possessed with devils. His life was under a siege. The evil spirit tormented him and drove him to the tombs, where he abode. He was naked and bound in fetters and chains most of his life. This man was so dangerous that no man was able to hold him. He was undoubtedly isolated by family and friends. They would have abandoned him because no one would want to associate with a mad fellow, especially one with this degree of insanity.

When he met Jesus, his story changed. The evil spirits in him could not withstand the presence of Christ therefore, they begged Him not to torment them. But Jesus would have nothing of their pleas. This man was delivered of the evil spirits and transformed. The people who knew him before could not believe their eyes. Luke 8:35 says *"Then they went out to see what was done; and came to Jesus, and found the man, out of whom the devils were departed, sitting at the feet of Jesus, clothed, and in his right mind: and they were afraid"*.

He was not possessed with one or two devils but legions (which means that more than a thousand evil spirits were in him). This man later became an evangelist, proclaiming the goodness of God. Check out *verse 39 "... And he went his way, and published throughout the whole city how great things Jesus had done unto him."*

His story was transformed from shame and reproach to glory.

10. **Mary Magdalene**- This lady was a harlot who lived in Galilee and was possessed by seven (7) evil spirits. She encountered her own transformation to a new being when she met Jesus. From that day she ministered unto Jesus. After her deliverance, she sought the Lord and anointed His feet with an Alabaster box of oil and washed His feet with the tears of her eyes. There is nowhere the gospel of Christ is preached that her name would not be mentioned. She played a vital role during and after the crucifixion of Christ.

The Bible records in John 20:1-18 that Mary Magdalene was the first to visit the tomb of Jesus and was the first to see Christ after His death, before He appeared to His disciples. *In verse 17 "Jesus saith unto her, Touch me not; for I am not yet ascended to my Father: but go to my brethren, and say unto them, I ascend unto my Father, and your Father: and to my God, and your God".*

All over the world, when the story of Christ's resurrection is being discussed, Mary Magdalene's name must surely be mentioned. This is a glorious testimony.

11. Saul of Tarsus (Apostle Paul)

– Saul of Tarsus was a man who single

handedly persecuted the early church. In Acts 8:3, it was recorded thus,

"As for Saul, he made havock of the church, entering into every house, and hailing men and women committed them to prison."

He was so notorious to the extent that anyone found preaching in the name of Christ was arrested. Saul worked for the devil mightily. All the while, God was silent because He saw a great man.

His divine encounter came in Acts 9:3-16, when the Spirit of God arrested him for persecuting the church. He was converted and immediately began to preach the gospel. Perhaps, we can say that Paul later because a versatile and uncompromising apostle that Israel ever produced.

Everywhere Paul went, he preached the gospel. He took the gospel of Christ to the uttermost part of the world in his time. And God used him mightily to the extent that handkerchiefs taken from his body were laid on the sick and they were made whole Act 19: 11-12. He was spirit-filled and through him many souls were won for the Lord.

He testified in Ephesians 3:8 that, "Unto me, who am less than the least of all saints, is this grace given, that I should preach among the Gentiles the unserchable riches of Christ;

In tribulations, in trials, in weariness and pain, with hunger and thirst, nakedness and fasting, he preached the gospel. Paul was gifted from above.

Now, the people we have examined above are Bible characters which all of us in our generation have only read about. We have not seen them but we believe the report to be true as it is written in the word of God. If we look around us, we will also see some people whom we can relate with and their transformation testimonies from story to glory. This goes to prove that our God is the same yesterday, today and forever.

To this end, the important thing anyone asking God for transformation to glory should do is to pray to God for His mercy. It is by the grace and mercy of God that a man can live a life of glory. Rom 9:15-16 says

"...I will have mercy on whom I will have mercy, and I will have compassion on whom I will have compassion. 16So then it is not of

him that willeth, nor of him that runneth, but of God that sheweth mercy."

A man cannot rely on his strength, ability and wisdom to manifest the glory of God (Proverbs 3:5-7). Moreover, before a man can experience transformation, his ways must be right with God. He must surrender his life to Jesus as his Lord and Savior. For *John 3: 3 says.*

"Verily, verily I say unto thee, Except a man be born again, he cannot see the kingdom of God".

It is the will of the Father, that all His bonafide children manifest His glory. Ask God to open your eyes to see what you need to do to change your life. May you experience divine transformation today in Jesus' unfailing name. (Amen)

Chapter Three: From Glory To Glory

"But we all, with unveiled face beholding as in a mirror the glory of the Lord, are being transformed into the same image from glory to glory, just as by the Spirit of the Lord."(II Corinthians 3:18 (NKJV)

The preceding chapter explains in details what it means for a story to transform into glory. The next question that may cross your mind is 'How can I move from the present level of glory I am?

God has many attributes, one of which is that He is unchangeable. Although He is unchangeable, stagnancy is definitely not one of his many attributes. This is evident in John 15:2 where He says *"Every branch in Me that beareth not fruit he taketh away and every branch that beareth fruit, he purgeth it, that it may bring forth more fruit.* God does not tolerate stagnancy. Taking a close look at the scriptures, we see that God is always moving His own people from one level of glory to the next so His name can be glorified. He is still in the business of doing that. Therefore, it is important to note that one thing that distinguishes a Prince from an ordinary citizen is the glory he carries. Without doubt, if you are God's own, His glory will distinguish you from unbelievers and even fellow believers.

It is very sad to observe that many Christians do not have a clear understanding of what it really means to move from one level of glory to the next. Often times, moving up is attributed to financial increase, material blessings, pleasure and worldly things. I will not be surprised if the aforementioned is also your concept of moving from glory to glory.

At this juncture, I will like to refer you back to. II Corinthians 3:18. What is Apostle Paul saying in that text?

It simply means becoming more and more like Jesus which is only possible through the work of the Holy Spirit that lives in us. Please take note of some salient words in the text- "Unveiled face". The phrase 'Unveiled face' as used by Paul in this text refers to the change in covenant i.e. the new covenant.

In the book of Exodus 33:12-23, Moses said to God, *'You said You have known Me by name and that I have also found grace in Your sight. If this is so, show me now your way, this will prove that I know you and have found grace in your sight'* (Paraphrased). In other words, Moses was asking God for a manifestation to back up what He had said concerning him. In response to his request,

God told him, *"My Presence will go with you, and I will give you rest."* Moses was not satisfied. He went on to say, *"If thy presence go not with me, carry us not up hence. 16 For wherein shall it be known here that I and thy people have found grace in thy sight? Is it not in that thou goest with us? So shall we be separated, I and thy people, from all the people that are upon the face of the earth."* God further reassured Moses, 17...I will also do this thing that you have spoken: for you have found grace in my sight and I have known you by name. (NKJV)

Moses was still satisfied, but not safe so he negotiated further," *...Please show me Your glory"* He specifically requested to see the glory of God. God again told him He would make all His goodness pass before Moses but he would not see his face as no man can see

His face and live. Moses was desperate for God's glory and he got it.

When Moses descended from Mount Sinai, his life had been transformed and the glory of God radiated around him. The heat was so much that, he did not know that his face shone while he talked with God. Aaron and all the children of Israel could not look directly at his face. Infact, they were terrified and could not approach him. Moses had to reach out to them so he could give them the commandments. He noticed the discomfort of the people and had to cover his face with a veil but whenever he was going to the Presence of God, he removed the veil.

"And when Aaron and all the Children of Israel saw Moses, the skin of his face shone, and they were afraid to come nigh him"

"And till Moses had done speaking with them, he put a veil on his face, But when Moses went in before the Lord to speak with Him, he took the veil off, until he came out. And he came out, and spake unto the children of Israel that which he was commanded.

"And the children of Israel saw the face of Moses, that the skin of Moses' face shone; and Moses put the veil upon his face again until he went in to speak with Him". Exodus {34:30-35}

Moses had a veil on because the children of Israel could not behold the evidence of the glory of God on him. Also, it is imperative to note that in Exodus 33:17-23, God identified Moses as His own.

"..... I know thee by name, and thou hast also found grace in my sight".

Exodus 33:12

The above text corroborates what I mentioned earlier, Moses was on a level of glory before he asked God for another level. God took Moses to the next level of glory because Moses was His own. The only reason why Aaron and all the Children of Israel could not behold the glory of God on Moses was because they had not been totally transformed to be like God. This is not to say that Moses did not have his lapses, but what distinguished him from the children of Israel was his WILLINGNESS to give up the lapses and his STRONG DESIRE to see God's glory.

Therefore, Paul is saying that now, we can behold the Glory of God in the face of Christ with an unveiled face just like Moses. The children of Israel did not behold God's glory directly. They beheld it through Moses and even then, they could not look at his face. He had to veil his face whenever he was with them. Because Moses was on a higher level of glory with God, whenever He was going to the presence of God, he went with an unveiled face. The only way through which we can be more and more like Christ is through the help of the Holy Spirit.

John Mac Arthur has this to say about moving from glory to glory.

"The new covenant; the gospel and message of Jesus Christ is clear. The light has been turned on and we can look with an unobstructed view right at the glory of God revealed in Christ; we are moved from one level of Glory to the next by the Holy Spirit; who is moving us into the image of the very glory we behold".

Moving from one level of glory to the next in our walk with God is what is called *PROGRESSIVE SANCTIFICATION*. This is Christian growth. It is the process of becoming like Christ as we gaze at the Glory of the Lord. In other words, moving from one level of glory to the next means a process of being transformed into the likeness of Jesus Christ. It is expected that we live to the glory of God and increasingly manifest it. By now, you may be wondering, if moving from one level of glory to the next only revolves around spiritual life?

Let's take a quick look at Matthew 6:33

"But seek ye first the kingdom of God, and his righteousness; and all these things be added unto you"

From the foregoing scripture we can deduce that when you increase in your spiritual life;

there will definitely be increase in other areas of your life. This is due to the fact that God HATES stagnancy. His desire for us is all-round glory. 3rd John 2 says, "Beloved, I wish above all things that thou mayest prosper and be in health, even as thy soul prospereth"

Now that we have an understanding of what it means to move from one level of Glory to the next, we move further to discuss the steps we are required to take in order to accomplish it.

Steps Required For Moving From Glory To Glory.

1. Trust God.

For you to move from glory to glory, you must trust the one that first of all placed you on the level you are presently. We honour God by trusting Him and when you honour God, you become more like Jesus.

"Blessed is the man that trusteth in the Lord, and whose hope the LORD is.[8] For he shall be as a tree planted by the waters, and that spreadeth out her roots by the river, and shall not see when heat   cometh, but her leaf shall be green; and shall not be careful in the   year of drought, never shall cease from yielding fruit". Jeremiah 17:7-8.

The above verses describe the advantage of trusting in God.

2. Have a relationship with the Holy Spirit.

Anyone who wishes to move from glory to glory must establish a relationship with the Holy Spirit. Such a person must be in constant fellowship with Him. The Holy Spirit is a

Teacher and He has the ability to teach all that one needs to know to attain the next level. To maintain the relationship with the holy Spirit

"But the comforter, which is the Holy Ghost, whom the father will send in my name, he shall teach you all things, and bring all things to your remembrance, whatsoever I have said unto you." John 14:26

But ye shall receive power, after that the Holy Ghost is come upon you: and ye shall be witnesses unto me both in Jerusalem, and in all Judaea, and in Samaria, and unto the uttermost part of the earth" Acts1:8

Many times, new converts or even Christians underestimate the power of the Holy Spirit. They perceive Him as a 'thing' rather than God. We should always have it at the back of our minds that it is only the Holy Spirit that can transform us into the image of Jesus

Christ. It is the Holy Spirit that can reveal the mind of God concerning all issues of life. The Holy Spirit is a personality and the third in the Trinity

3. Study the Word of God.

This must be taken seriously. The word of God must be highly esteemed for any believer to move from glory to glory. The Bible says in Matthew 4:4 that, "...*Man shall not live by bread alone, but by every word that proceedeth out of the mouth of God.*" Gold is not found on the streets, and treasures are not displayed in open spaces. In the same way, power, knowledge and wisdom to move to glory are embedded in the word of God – the Bible and that is why 2Tim.2:15 enjoin us to study the word

4. Believe the word of God

We must take God's word as the final authority over any matter. Whatever the Word says concerning an issue that is what it is. It is settled. When we doubt, the word doesn't work for us. Take for example the case of Abraham and Sarah. When Sarah doubted, Abraham trusted the word of God and it eventually worked for them.

"He staggered not at the promise of God through unbelief; but was strong in faith giving glory to God". Romans 4:20

No matter how terrible or impossible the situation may be, we should never question the integrity of God's word or doubt it. Take for example the three (3) Hebrew boys; Shadrach, Meshach, and Abednego. They refused to bow down to Nebuchadnezzar's god. I love to quote their reply to king

Nebuchadnezzar when he queried their refusal to bow.

"If it be so, our God whom we serve is able to deliver us from the burning fiery furnace, and he will deliver us out of thine hand, O king.

But if not, be it known unto thee, O king, that we will not serve thy gods, nor worship the golden image which thou hast set up".

Daniel 3:17-18

The three young men stood for God even in the face of a fiery furnace. How many of us can stand for Jesus Christ today in the midst of this corrupt generation? Shadrach, Meshach and Abednego trusted God's word. Even if they had died on account of their dogged trust in God, they knew He would take them to glory.

In summary, if we do not trust God, we make Him a liar. Let us consider 1 John 5:10.

"He that believeth on the Son of God hath the witness in himself: he that believeth not God hath made him a liar; because he believeth not the record that God gave of his Son."

5. Live your life to the glory of God

Many Christians find it difficult to live their lives to the glory of God alone. They seek to impress their spouses, family, friends, relationship dreams, ambitions and self. These entities are not bad in themselves and may seem difficult to abandon for something we cannot see but the fact remains that God is the architect of them all and only deserves to be glorified. Jesus, our perfect example always glorified God for everything He did on earth.

"And I seek not mine own glory: there is one that seeketh and judgeth".

John 8:50

It is imperative to know that living our lives solely to glorify God is a command from God. Let us take a look at 1 Corinthians 10:31

"Whether therefore ye eat, or drink, or whatsoever ye do, do all to the glory of God". 1 Corinthians 10:31

Paul used eating or drinking, as an allegory to explain that we should glorify God in everything that we do. John Macarthur's opinion on this goes thus:

"Let me put it to you and may be give it some richer content. As mundane as eating and drinking, that becomes the focal point of everything you do in your life. That has to be the all consuming direction of your life i.e.

you are never going to do anything willfully and knowingly that does not bring honour to God."

'If any man come to me, and hate not his father, and mother, and wife, and children, and brethren, and sisters, yea, and his own life also, he cannot be my disciple. And whosoever doth not bear his cross, and come after me, cannot be my disciple. For which of you, intending to build a tower, sitteth not down first and counteth the cost, whether he have sufficient to finish it? Lest haply,   after he hath laid the foundation, and is not able to finish it, all that behold it begin to mock him, Saying, This man began to build, and was not able to finish.

Luke: 14:26-30

Firstly, being devoted to living solely to the glory of God may make one lose ones family and friends or even lives. It cost Stephen, James and Peter their lives.

Secondly, living to glorify God means self-sacrifice. One may be required to give up your life as explained in the passage above. Your life here may be your family, ambition, dreams or goals. To move from one level of glory to the next means to be a selfless Christian. Jesus Christ was selfless, that was why He died to save the world.

Lastly, when you live your life solely to the glory of God, be ready to suffer with Christ. Peter always told the Church to rejoice when they suffered with Christ.

"Yet if any man suffer as a Christian, let him not be ashamed; but let him glorify God on this behalf." 1 Peter 4:16

"They were stoned, they were sawn asunder, were tempted, were slain with the sword: they wondered about in sheepskins and goat skin; being destitute, afflicted, tormented;"
Hebrew 11:37

6. Be ready to suffer persecution.

There is no gold without fire and no salvation without sacrifice. Jesus Christ paid a great price with his life to save humanity. In spite of his righteousness and good works, He was dishonored, confronted, attacked, condemned and crucified. In the same vein, be ready to suffer persecution from glory attackers. Like Jesus, have zero tolerance for anything that dishonors God and remain focused

".And found in the temple those that sold oxen and sheep and doves, and the changers of money sitting: And when He had made a scourge of small cords, he drove them all out

of the temple, and the sheep, and the oxen;, and poured out the changer's money, and overthrew the tables;

And said unto them that sold doves, Take these things hence; make not my Father's house a house of merchandise. And his disciples remembered that it was written, The Zeal of thine house hath eaten Me up". John 2:14 – 17

From the above passage, we understand the impact of defending God. Like Jesus, we should feel hurt when unbelievers defile God and be ready to defend Him

7. Be a man of prayer and praise.

For you to move from one level of glory to the next, you must be a man of prayer and praise. By this I mean that you must devote quality time for praying and praising God. David turned himself to an encyclopedia of His attributes. Let us take a look at Psalm 50: 23, 86: 9 -12.

"Whoso offereth praise glorifieth me: and to him that ordereth his conversation aright will I shew the salvation of God". Psalm 50:23.

"All nations whom thou hast made shall come and worship before thee, O Lord; and shall glorify thy name.₁₀. For thou art great, and doest wondrous things: thou art God alone.

Teach me thy way, O Lord; I will walk in thy truth: unite my heart to fear thy name. I will praise thee, O Lord my God, with all my heart: and I will glorify thy name for evermore". Psalm 86: 9 – 12

The importance of praise and worship cannot be over-emphasized. Praise and worship God in every situation, good or bad. Learn to always give thanks to God as the Psalmist says:

"It is a good thing to give thanks unto the Lord, and to sing praises unto thy name, O Most High." Psalm 92:1

"God is a Spirit: and they that worship him must worship him in Spirit and in truth". John 4:24.

When we worship God, it is good to enumerate His wonderful works, in your life and in Bible time. Let's go to the book of Habakkuk in order to have a clearer understanding.

"God came from Teman, and the Holy One from mount Paran. Selah. His glory covered the heavens and the earth was full of his praise.

And His brightness was as the light; he had horns coming out of his hand: and there was the hiding of his power. Before Him went the pestilence and burning coals went forth at His feet.

He stood, and measured the earth: he beheld, and drove asunder the nations; and the everlasting mountains were scattered, the perpetual hills did bow: his ways are everlasting. I saw the tents of Cushan in affliction: and the curtains of the land of Midian did tremble.

Habakkuk 3:3-7

"God is our refuge and strength, a very present help in trouble".

Psalm 46:1

"Lord, thou hast been our dwelling place in all generations." Psalm 90:1

"O worship the Lord in the beauty of holiness: fear before him, all the earth". Psalm 96:9

Again, when we praise God, we must remember to thank Him for every single deed, no matter how little. We should thank Him for His wonderful works as well as His attributes. When you do this constantly with love, you are definitely moving from one level of glory to the next.

"Unto him be glory in the Church by Christ Jesus throughout all ages, world without end. Amen." Ephesians 3:21

When we pray to God, we are enhancing our relationship with Him. Also, we should always confess our sins during prayers. This is owing to the fact that unforgiven sin can lead to stagnancy or delay of glory. It is also imperative to restitute when necessary in order to avoid all loopholes the devil may capitalize on

"He that covereth his sins shall not prosper: but whoso confesseth them and forsaketh them shall have mercy." Proverbs 28:13.

8. Be fruitful

This is a very important point. Fruitfulness is key in our walk with God. Jesus Christ taught on the importance of being fruitful in the book of John. Let us take a good look at John 15: 1-2.

"I am the true vine, and my father is the husband man. Every branch in me that beareth not fruit he taketh away: and every branch that beareth fruit, he purgeth it that it may bring forth more fruit." John 15:1-2

Now, let me take the foregoing a little deeper. You cannot claim to be born again if the people around you are not positively influenced or blessed by you.

"Herein is my Father glorified, that ye bear much fruit, so shall ye be my disciples." John 15:8

The above verse corroborates the aforementioned. For God's glory to continue to grow in your life, you need to be fruitful. When you are fruitful, it means you become more and more like Jesus Christ. It is important to say that Jesus Christ was very fruitful, he won many souls, delivered many from satanic bondage and healed countless of people.

If Jesus Christ had not influenced and taught the twelve disciples and the Apostles who passed on the message of salvation on, it was documented; there might have been no evidence of his life today.

Another aspect of being fruitful is possessing and exhibiting the fruit of the Holy Spirit. Many Christians want to move from one level of glory to the next, yet they have attitude problem. They are untidy, impatient and quick to anger; harbor hatred and keep malice. Let us see what Philippians 1:11 has to say.

"Being filled with the fruits of righteousness, which are by Jesus Christ, unto the glory and praise of God." Philippians 1:11

Being fruitful also includes walking your talk. Many Christians do not practice what they preach. That was the problem the Pharisees and the Scribes had. They were quick to correct others and loved to be called "Rabbi". More or less, "Mr. Goody two shoes. "Meanwhile, they were worse than those they corrected. Jesus called them *HYPROCRITES*.

Paul in his letter to the Romans shed some light on the issue.

"Thou therefore which teachest another, teachest thou not thyself? Thou that preachest a man should not steal, dost thou steal? Thou that sayest a man should not commit adultery? thou that abhorest idols, dost thou commit sacrilege? Thou that makest thy boast of the law, through breaking the law dishonourest thou God? For the name of God is blasphemed among the gentiles through you, as it is written.

Romans 2:21-24

The verses are self-explanatory. Many Christians at that time did not exhibit the fruit of the spirit and they were hypocrites. Consequently, the name of God was being mocked and blasphemed among the gentiles.

The Jews lacked good works and righteousness.

Furthermore, John MacArthur identifies two types of fruits – Action fruit and Attitude Fruit. First, action fruit means what you do, your righteous deeds. Take for example leading people to Jesus Christ, giving people in need, etc. Let's consider Romans 1:13 and Philippians 4:17.

"Now I will not have you ignorant, brethren, that oftentimes I purposed to come unto you, (but was let hitherto,) that I might have some fruit among you also, even as among other gentiles." Romans 1:13

Here, Paul refers to anticipated believers as fruits.

"Not because I desire a gift: But I desire fruit that may abound to your account." Philippians 4:17

Also, an action fruit includes any kind of righteous praise to God and any manifestation of God in your life. Let us see Colossians 1:10.

"That ye might walk worthy of the Lord unto all pleasing, being fruitful in every good work, and increasing in the knowledge of God;"

The second type of fruit identified by John MacArthur is the attitude fruit. Behind the action fruit is the attitude fruit. As we stated earlier, the fruit of the spirit is part of being fruitful. If you walk in the spirit, the spirit will produce attitude fruit. This attitude fruit results in action fruit, and when your life is characterized by more fruit, you will move from one level of glory to the next.

Chapter Four: The Pain of Lost Glory

Having discussed extensively on how to move from one level of glory to the next, it is imperative that we know that glory can be lost.

Recall that in the preceding chapter, we identified some steps that enhance moving from one level of glory to the next. When an individual jettison any of those moves, glory can be lost.

If Samson had an opportunity to write his autobiography, the literature will win many souls. If Saul could turn the hand of time, he would not only destroy the Amalekites, but bomb the entire city to extinction. Many people in the Bible lost their glory due to one sin or the other.

Do not think that because we are in the era of grace, it is therefore impossible to lose one's glory. I am most delighted to inform you that God is a God of standard and principle. He is unchangeable and so are His words. He does not go back on His words and He is not going to break the rules. He says in the Book of Ecclesiastes 10:8.

"He that diggeth a pit shall fall into it; and whoso breaketh an hedge, a serpent shall bite him"

God is aware that people have a tendency to fall. Even Jesus, in His letter to the church in Ephesus, warned them to return to their first love and remember where they had fallen. By this, He meant that they should return to the level of glory they used to be. Let us take a quick look at the scriptures:

"Remember therefore from whence thou art fallen, and repent, and do the first works; or else I will come unto thee quickly, and will remove thy candlestick out of his place, except thou repent" Revelation 2:5

Now, we move further to examine some characters in the bible that lost their glory due to sin. As we go along, note the kind of vice that led to the loss of glory.

Some biblical examples of those who lost their glory

1. **Adam**- This was the first man God created and the first to lose his glory. The second creator was also the second to the glory. The couple experienced the first hand glory of God but , they lost it as a result of

disobedience. The Oxford Advanced Learner's Dictionary defines disobedience as: ***"Failing and refusing to obey."***

God gave Adam a simple instruction not to eat of the fruit of a particular tree. When the instruction was flouted, they realized their fallen state and God had a conversation with them:

"And he said, who told thee that thou wast naked? Hast thou eaten of the tree, whereof I commanded thee that thou shouldest not eat? And the man said, the woman whom thou gaveth to be with me, she gave me of the tree, and I did eat." Genesis 3:11-12

After this incident, God expelled them from the Garden of Eden. *"And the*

Lord God said, Behold, the man is become as one of us, to know good and evil: and now, lest he put forth his hand, and take also of the tree of life, and eat, and live forever: Therefore the Lord God sent him forth from the Garden of Eden, to till the ground from whence he was taken" Genesis 3:22-23

Adam and Eve enjoyed direct fellowship with God prior to their expulsion but at their disobedience, they lost their glory and fellowship.

The loss of their glory was that of the entire human race and it cost God the death of His only begotten son to restore it.

2. **Saul**- Another biblical character who lost his glory as a result of

disobedience was Saul. Just like Adam, God gave Saul an instruction to destroy everything in a particular city. Let us take a quick look at the scripture.

"₁Samuel also said unto Saul, The LORD sent me to anoint thee to be king over his people, over Israel: now therefore hearken thou unto the voice of the words of the LORD.

Thus saith the LORD of hosts, I remember that which Amalek did to Israel, how he laid wait for him in the way, when he came up from Egypt. Now go and smite Amalek, and utterly destroy all that they have, and spare them not; but slay man and woman, infant and suckling, ox and sheep, camel and ass." 1 Samuel 15:1-3

In the above verses, God gave Saul an instruction. Go with me to the next verses and see what Saul did.

"But Saul and the people spared Agag, and the best of the sheep, and of the oxen, and of the fatlings, and the lambs, and all that was good, and would not utterly destroy them: but every thing that was   vile   and refuse, that they destroyed utterly."

Genesis 15:9

Knowing fully well the instruction of God, Saul still went ahead to satisfy his own desires. Many Christians know the mind of God concerning some issues but   because of a fat salary, pretty wife and worldly pleasures, they ignore the word of God to satisfy themselves. This often leads to loss of glory.

3. Gehazi & Judas Iscariot- These duo lost their glory due to greed. The Oxford Advanced Learner's Dictionary defines Greed as: *"A strong desire for more food or drink when you are no longer thirsty or hungry"*. A study of the characters of Gehazi and Judas can fully explain this vice. Gehazi's desire for material wealth fits the definition given overleaf. He was on a particular level of glory by virtue of his position as a servant to Elisha. Perhaps he would have got a double portion of Elisha's anointing if he had been contended and upright. Let us take a look at 2 Kings 5:20-27

"But Gehazi, the servant of Elisha the man of God, said, Behold my master hath spared Naaman this Syrian, in not receiving at his hands   that which he brought: but as the LORD liveth, I will run after him, and take somewhat of him. So Gehazi followed after Naaman. And when Naaman saw him running after him, he lighted down from the Chariot to meet him, and said, is all well?

And he said, All is well. My master hath sent me, saying, Behold, even now there be come to me from mount Ephraim two young men of the sons of the prophets: give them, I pray thee, a talent of silver, and two changes of garments.

And Naaman said, Be content, take two talents. And he urged him, and bound two talents of silver in two bags, with two changes of garments, and laid them upon two of his servants; and they bare them before him.

And when he came to the tower, he took them from their hand, and bestowed them in the house: and he let the men go, and they departed.

But he went in, and stood before his master. And Elisha said unto him, whence comest thou, Gehazi? And he said, thy servant went no whither. And he said unto him, Went not mine heart with thee, when the man turned again from his chariot to meet thee? Is it a time to receive money, and to receive garments, and olive yards, and vineyards, and sheep, and oxen, and men servants, and maid servants?

The Leprosy therefore of Naaman shall cleave unto thee, and unto thy seed forever. And he went out from his presence a leper as white as snow ."

Often times, Christians have lost their glory as a result of greed. The scenario may not play out like what happened in the case of Gehazi and the repercussion may be totally different as well but the fact remains that there is a punishment for a greedy man. Even King Solomon in the Book of Proverbs warned against greed.

"He that is greedy of gain troubleth his own house; but he that hateth gifts shall live." Proverb 15:27

"Treasures of wickedness profit nothing: but righteousness delivereth from death." Proverb 10:2

In the case of Judas Iscariot, his desire was his personal well-being. He did not care what happened to his master Jesus. He sold him for only thirty pieces of silver. Many Christians today have sold their wives, husbands, children, family, friends and even the Church for money or material gain. Like Judas, such individuals will eventually lose their glory. Greed is common among church leaders. Some pastors dictate the amount they want as honorarium, the kind of accommodation, etc. They seem to forget their primary assignment and the salvation was not bought by money and should not be sold Judas lost his glory and was replaced by another disciple. What a shame!

Whenever you are tempted by greed, remember the fate of Gehazi and Judas Iscariot. Gehazi brought a curse not only upon himself but generations after him. Judas Iscariot ended up committing suicide, thereby losing eternal life as there was no record to show that he repented before he died. Resist any temptation to be greedy.

4. **King Nebuchadnezzar & Queen Vashti-** Another vice to avoid is PRIDE. It is a very great sin in the sight of God. It top the lists of vices according to Proverbs 6:16. Because

God made us who we are, any act that ascribes glory to us rather than God is a sin of Pride. The Oxford Advanced Learner's Dictionary defines pride as: *"A feeling of respect that you have for yourself."* Or

"The feeling that you are better or more important than other people."

Let us first examine King Nebuchadnezzar. Despite the warning God gave him through Daniel, he felt that all he had was by his power. His refusal to acknowledge God's place in his life cost him his position for a while. Let us go through book of Daniel.

"While the word was in the king's mouth, there fell a voice from heaven saying, O king Nebuchadnezzar, to

thee it is spoken; The kingdom is departed from thee.

And they shall drive thee from men, and thy dwelling shall be with beasts of the field. They shall make thee to eat grass as oxen, and seven times shall pass over thee, until thou know that the most High ruleth in the kingdom of men, and giveth it to whosoever he will.

The same hour was the thing fulfilled upon Nebuchadnezzar; and he was driven from men, and did eat grass as oxen, and his body was wet with the dew of heaven, till his hairs were grown like eagles' feathers, and his nails like birds' claws." Daniel 4:31-33.

King Nebuchadnezzar lost his glory and was reduced to the level of an animal. Although he later on regained his human mind the bad record can never be erased. It has been passed from one generation to the next.

Queen Vashti is another character who lost her glory as a result of pride. Although many theologians opine that king Ahasuerus was wrong to have demanded that she displayed her beauty. That notwithstanding, her manner of approach to the request was a display of pride. Go with me quickly to the book of Esther.

"On the seventh day, when the heart of the king was merry with wine, he commanded   Mehuman,   Biztha,

Harbona, Bigtha, and Abagtha, Zethar and Carcas, the seven chamberlains that served in the presence of Ahasuerus the king.To bring Vashti the Queen before the king with the crown royal, to shew the people and the princes her beauty: for she was fair to look on. But the Queen Vashti refused to come at the king's commandment by his chamberlains: therefore was the king very wroth, and his anger burned in him." Esther 1: 10-12.

The consequence of her reaction was her removal as queen.

"If it please the king, let there go a royal commandment from him, and let it be written among the laws of the Persians and the Medes, that it be not

altered, That Vashti come no more before king Ahasuerus; and let the king give her royal estate unto another that is better than she." Esther 1:19.

We learn from the stories of king Nebuchadnezzar and Queen Vashti that pride goes before a fall. One major observation about the two characters is that they both held royal positions. We can therefore say that perhaps their position got into their heads. They forgot that all power that be, comes from God. Proverbs 16:5 says, *"Everyone that is proud in heart is an abomination to the LORD: though hand join in hand, he shall not be unpunished"*

For King Nebuchadnezzar, pride coupled with disobedience made him loose his glory. Queen Vashti on the other hand allowed pride and her beauty to rob her of her glory.

5. **Samson & King Solomon**-Any kind of sin can rob a man of his glory. Using the characters of Samson and Solomon, let us identify the vice that made them lose their glory.

Samson was a strong man, a mighty man of valour, but he loved women. The sin of fornication robbed him of his glory. His enemy used this vice against him and he was de-glorified.

"And it came to pass afterward, that he loved a woman in the

valley of Sorek, whose name was Delilah.

And the lords of the Philistine came up unto her, and said unto her, Entice him and see wherein his great strength lieth, and by what means we may prevail against him, that we may bind him to afflict him; and we will give thee every one of us eleven hundred pieces of silver." Judges 16:4-5.

He totally enjoyed the attention and company of this strange woman to the extent that even when she kept pestering him for the secret of his strength, did not discern that she was a threat. This was how Samson was captured into the Philistine's camp. Samson, who had been a threat to them, became an entertainer and a laughing stock all of a sudden. He lost his glory on the laps of Delilah. He was carried away by lust and lost all sensitivity. Many Christians have lost their glory as a result of fornication and adultery.

Let me quickly take you to the book of Hebrews.

"Lest there be any fornicator, or profane person, as Esau, who for one morsel of meat sold his birthright. For ye know how that afterward, when he would have inherited the blessing, he was rejected: for he found no place of repentance, though he sought it carefully with tears." Hebrews 12: 16-17

From the above verses, we can deduce that the portion that aptly describes what Samson did is called, profanity. He despised the uncommon grace of God upon his life and eventually lost it due to fornication. Fornication is a great destroyer, so BEWARE!

The great king Solomon, the wisest man that ever lived, lost his glory as a result of adultery. He loved many strange women. The Bible records in 1 Kings 11:3 that, *"And he had seven hundred wives, princesses, and three hundred concubines: and his wives turned away his heart."* The temple he built for God was eventually destroyed.

6. Cain, Korah, Dathan and Abiram

The first man on the earth to commit

the sin of envy was Cain. He allowed the spirit of envy to consume him when God accepted and preferred the sacrifice of his brother, Abel but rejected his own. The envy grew into hatred and it finally led to murder. Cain therefore, lost his glory and was cursed by God. *"₁₁And now art thou cursed from the earth, which hath opened her mouth to receive thy brother's blood from thy hand;*

When thou tillest the ground, it shall not henceforth yield unto thee her strength; a fugitive and a vagabond shall thou be in the earth." Genesis 4:11-12.

The Oxford Advanced Learner's Dictionary defines envy as: *"The feeling of wanting to be in the same situation as somebody else and the feeling of wanting something that somebody else has."*

Just like the dictionary defines envy, some Christians always desire to want something that somebody else has. It may be position, power, wife, husband, etc. As Christians, we must fight against the spirit of envy. Korah, Dathan and Abiram also lost their glory because they envied Moses.

"Now Korah, the son of Izhar, the son of Kohath, the son of Levi and Dathan and Abiram, the sons of Eliab, and On, the son of Peleth, sons of Reuben, took men. And they rose up before Moses, with certain of the children of Israel, two hundred and fifty princes of the assembly, famous in the

congregation, men of renown."
Numbers 16:1-2.

They felt that God should use them as He did Moses so the ganged up against him but God defended Moses.

"But if the LORD make a new thing, and the earth open her mouth and swallow them up, with all that appertain unto them, and they go down quick into the pit; then ye shall understand that these men have provoked the LORD." Numbers 16:30.

We can go discussing men who lost their glory in the Bible. May we never lose our glory. Let us endeavour to always to live in accordance to the word of God.

Chapter Five: Recovering Lost Glory

Having established in the previous chapters that the glory of God can actually be on a man, as it was with Moses (Exodus 33:12-23) and that it is also possible for the glory to be lost, does this preclude that there is no solution?

I make bold to say that no matter what might have happened in the past, there is hope. The Bible expressly states in the book of Job 14:7, *"For there is hope of a tree, if it be cut down, that it will sprout again, and that the tender branch thereof will not cease."* After the incidence that happened in the Garden of Eden whereby man lost his glory, God began making preparation for the restoration which came through Jesus Christ. In the case of Nebuchadnezzar, we also see that God restored his glory as recorded in Daniel 4:34-37. Let us take a look at verse 36,

"At the same time my reason returned unto me; and for the glory of my kingdom, mine honour and brightness returned unto me; and my counselors and my lords sought unto me; and I was established in my kingdom, and excellent majesty was added unto me."

What a glorious God! The story of king Nebuchadnezzar changed and he returned, blessed, praised and honored God, acknowledging that His dominion is everlasting and His kingdom is from generation to generation. He agreed that man is nothing before God and that God is unquestionable. You will notice here that, his restoration began when he addressed the issue that caused him to lose the glory in the first place.

For glory to be restored, we must act in accordance to the word of God as stated in 1 Chronicles 16:29. *"Give unto the LORD, the glory due unto his name: bring an offering, and come before him: worship the LORD in the beauty of holiness"*. We can also consider 1 Corinthians 6:20 *"For ye are bought with a price: therefore glorify God in your body and in your spirit, which are God's"*. Whether it be by life or by death, Christ must be magnified in our body. (Philippians 1:20).

If we consider the case of Samson, the Bible says in Judges 16:20 that"... *And he awoke out of his sleep, and said, I will go out as at other times before and shake myself. And he wist not that the LORD was departed from him"* Samson did not realize that he had lost his glory until when he shook himself as he used to and nothing happened. What a pathetic story! This was a man that was dedicated to

God from birth. An angel heralded his conception and gave guidelines as to how he was to be raised. He rent a young lion that roared against him, single-handedly killed thirty(30) men, caught three hundred(300) foxes, slew a thousand(1,000) men with the jawbone of an ass, carried on his shoulders the doors of the gate of a city with the two posts and took them up on a hill. When he was bound with new ropes, he broke free with ease. The Bible says, "...*he brake them off his arms like a thread*". However, on the fateful day, he woke up like all other days when he killed a lion, slew a thousand men, etc. but alas! The power behind him was no more. God had departed from him and his glory was no more.

It is obvious that many of us may have lost the glory and it is still unknown to us because we still call on His name and join other believers to serve Him not knowing that His presence is no longer with us. It is therefore important for us to know how to recover a lost glory. Samson was on the path to recovery when his hair began to grow again and in that state, he called upon God, asking Him for strength so he could avenge the Philistines for his plucked eyes. Imagine that! He had an opportunity for a second chance and his only concern was to avenge. Many people seem to have extremely narrow, partial and obscure view of God. They are so shadow-like and dim in their notion of Him. Many of us are somewhat in this condition and this could also be the reason for not being fulfilled.

May we be wise Christians and may we enjoy total restoration in Jesus name.

How Do We Recover Lost Glory?

1. Glorify God in all things.

God calls us to glorify Him in all that we do. We see the call to glorify God in many verses of the scriptures.

"Ye that fear the LORD, praise Him; all ye the seed of Jacob, glorify him; and fear him, all ye seed of Israel". Psalm 22:23

The same call is made in Psalm 29:1-2,

"Give unto the Lord, O ye mighty, give unto the LORD glory and strength. ₂Give unto the Lord the glory due unto his name; worship the LORD in the beauty of holiness".

We are to glorify God in everything we do. It is also good to acknowledge, declare and value the glory of God in our lives. It is in magnifying God's glory that we can recover all we have lost. The heavens declare the glory of the Lord (Psalm 19:1) always and that is what we are called to do (1 Corinthians 10:31). To have our lost glory recovered, we must fulfill the responsibility we are given to declare, to make known, to reflect, to display the glory of God that He possesses.

To glorify God is to set Him highest in our thoughts and to have a venerable esteem of him like King Nebuchadnezzar did in Daniel 4:34 when his glory was restored to him.

Why must we glorify God to recover our glory?

a. **Because he gives us our being.** Psalm 100:3, "*Know ye that the LORD he is God: it is he that hath made us and not we ourselves; we are his people, and the sheep of his pasture*". If we all receive from his bounty, is it not reasonable that we should glorify him? Should we not live to Him, saying we live by Him as it is written in Romans 11:36?

b. **Because God has made all things for himself.** Proverbs 16:4 says" *"The LORD hath made all things for himself: yea, even the wicked for the day of evil."* Everything God has made will accomplish his glory.

c. **Because creatures below us, and above us, bring glory to God.** Psalm 19:1."*The heavens declare the glory of God and the firmament sheweth his handywork"*. Shall man be an exception? Isaiah 43:20," The beasts of the field, the dragons and owls honour God. Even angels bring glory to God, how much more, we, who have been dignified with honour above angelic spirits?

2. Abhor sin.

Living in sin is a rejection of God's glory. This is what makes sin so heinous, as Paul describes in Romans 1 and in verse 21,

"Because that, when they knew God, they glorified Him not as God, neither were thankful; but became vain in their imaginations and their foolish heart was darkened".

They knew the glorious God but rejected that knowledge. Choosing to follow foolish desires rather than glorifying Him as God. By refusing to align their thinking and affection and live with the truth and reality of all that He is, they became fools and lost their glory because they exchanged the worship of God the creator for the worship of the creature. (v.25)

People choose to sin because in those moments they believe lies rather than the truth. At the moment of temptation, a person is convinced that the way of disobedience to God is the best. This is exactly what happened to Eve in Genesis 3 and the glory of God departed from zero. The whole existence of man is to glorify God as GOD. Therefore, we must make a conscious effort to reject sin in order to recover the lost glory.

3. Delight in God's glory

For a lost glory to be recovered, we must actively engage ourselves in glorifying God. We do it by showing the worth and value of the Lord by the way we live. We must delight in God above all things. The glory of King Nebuchadnezzar was not given back to him until he acknowledged God and delighted in His glory. Daniel 4:37. For us to recover fully, we must see and appreciate the infinite worth of all that God is to us and does for us. The Christian life is not a charade. It is not a call to pretend to be pious by saying and doing the right things. It is a call to see and believe the truth and know that Man cannot and must not live outside the glory of God.

Paul, the Apostle delighted in God's glory and that helped him to willingly give up everything in order to know Him. Philippians 3:10. He was drenched in the glory of God that was revealed in Jesus Christ. All the things that he once boasted in, that he had judged to be of great worth, he later regarded as worthless in comparison to Jesus.

"But what things were gain to me, those I counted loss for Christ. ₈Yea doubtless, and I

count all things but loss for the excellency of the knowledge of Christ Jesus my Lord: for whom I have suffered the loss of all things, and do count them but dung, that I may win Christ" (Philippians 3:7-8).

It is only when we delight in God's glory that recovery is guaranteed. For this to happen, we must prefer God's glory above all other things. We must be contented with the will of God, confess sin, believe God and His words and work out our own salvation.

Sustaining the Recovered Glory

When glory is recovered, it is important that the beneficiary sustain it. In the book of Daniel, there is no record of a recurrence of what King Nebuchadnezzar did. This is because he realized that God's works are truth, his way is judgment and he is able to abase those that walk in pride. Therefore, as wise Christians, we need to know what do to ensure that the glory of God on us is sustained.

1. **Remain obedient:** A man who is totally obedient to the law of God will not live in sin. It must be noted that the deceit of sin must not be underestimated. So, we must not be carried away in sin, especially the pleasures it offers. Rather, we should find strength by pursuing greater pleasures that are offered us in Jesus Christ. Psalm 16:11 says, *"Thou wilt shew me the path of life: in thy presence is fullness of joy; at thy right hand there are pleasures for evermore".*

Psalm 36:8 says that God has a "river of pleasures" from which He draws deep, life-giving joy by which he provides refreshments for all His saints. Yes, sin has its own pleasure but God has a river of pleasures. If we go hard after those pleasures, we will magnify the glory of God and sustain it in our lives.

2. **Stay under the grace of God:** An example of a man that stayed under the grace of God is Noah. Staying under God's grace sustains the glory of God upon a man's life. God gave Noah specific instructions as to how the ark was to be constructed, even at a time when there was no record of rain. God asked him to take the animals with him to the ark. He never questioned the instructions but

obeyed to the letters. People jeered at him but he was sustained by grace. He stayed put in the ark until the set time when God allowed them to leave the ark. You will notice that in Genesis 7:16, it is recorded that God himself shut the ark. *"And they that went in, went in male and female of all flesh, as God had commanded him: and the LORD shut him in."* Noah had done his part by being obedient to God and the rest was a function of grace. In spite of everything that was going on around them, Noah, his family and the animals were shut in and kept by the grace of God. Note the way the Bible describe it. The waters prevailed, increased greatly, the waters prevailed exceedingly, all flesh upon the face of the earth died. But you know what?

They were securely shut in. May God shut us out of all temptations around us in Jesus name. Amen.

3. **Live by the Word of God:** Nothing but the undiluted word of God can reveal His glory to man. No intellectual acumen, no strength of logic, nothing at all but His word. Joshua 1:8 says, *"This book of the law shall not depart out of thy mouth; but thou shalt meditate therein day and night, that thou mayest observe to do according to all that is written therein: for then thou shall make thy way prosperous, and then thou shalt have good success"*.

It is clear here that the only way to remain in God's glory is to keep His word. The word of God is the lamp unto your feet and the light unto your path. Psalm 119:105. A man who walks in the light cannot stumble, and a man whose light has been recovered cannot be overshined by darkness. When the word of God is hidden in our hearts, it is impossible to sin against God (Psalm 119:11) and more so, the wisdom and understanding of God shall come upon us. (Proverbs 2:1-7).Even Jesus affirmed this in Matthew 4:4 when he said, *"...Man shall not live by bread alone, but by every word that proceedeth out of the mouth of God."*

4. **Fight the good fight of faith:** A man needs a stubborn faith to claim his glory, 1Timothy 6:12. We are to persevere in order to possess and retain our glory, Hebrews 6:12. All

those who retained their glory all through the Bible were men and women who had absolute faith in God and in His promises. Hebrews 11:1-11. They include the likes of Abel, Enoch, Noah, Abraham; the father of faith, Sarah, Moses and a host of others. Holding on to our faith in Him is paramount as no one can please Him without it. It is by faith that the impossible can become possible. In the story of Moses in Exodus, the red sea parted ways. For Joshua, the walls of Jericho fell down at a great shout. Just like Paul had the confidence in 2 Timothy 4:7, we must also fight the good fight of faith to the very end that we may also receive the crown of righteousness.

5. Rely on the Holy Spirit: It is important for anyone who wants to sustain His glory to rely on the Holy Spirit for help. John 14:16. Recovered glory may be lost forever if a man fails to acknowledge the power of the presence of the Holy Spirit. The truth about God can only be communicated through the Holy Spirit John 14:17 says, *"Even the Spirit of truth, whom the world cannot receive, because it seeth him not, neither knoweth him: but ye know him; for he dwelleth with you, and shall be in you"*. The Holy Spirit is the teacher of the bible. John 16:13. He will even teach you the truth about yourself; if you ask him. David was so refreshingly honest in Psalm 19:12 when he asked the Lord, *"Who* *can understand his errors? Cleanse thou me from secret faults".*

No one can fully discern his errors, but as we listen to the voice of the Holy Spirit and follow his promptings, the areas in our lives that are invisible to us will be refined and sublimated by the Holy Spirit.

"But we all, with open face beholding as in a glass the glory of the Lord, are changed into the same image from glory to glory, even as by the Spirit of the Lord." (2 Corinthians3:18)

It is by the Holy Spirit that we are liberated from sin and for service. Proverbs 1:23.

Chapter Six: A Stone Shall Not Replace Me; Use Me Oh Lord

God, who is able to do all things, desires that His beauty; which is His glory be revealed through us. This can be achieved if and only if we do that which pleases him.

This chapter throws more light on why we need to work and walk our ways into expressing the glory of God. It helps us to humble ourselves before God making us to solely understand that when a Christian fails or refuses to offer himself ready for the work of God, there are a million and one other people who are able and ready to take up the responsibility. These people become replacements for the lazy or weak ones. Even when and where there are none, God can raise stones to replace them. Despite the fact that we were made to occupy different spaces and fulfill various dreams, we are all dispensable. Only God is indispensable.

In Ecclesiastes 1:4 the Bible says, "*One generation passeth away, and another generation cometh: but the earth abideth for ever*". Verse 7 of the same chapter says, "*All the rivers run into the sea; yet the sea is not full; unto the place from whence the rivers come, thither they return again*". And in verse 11, "*There is no remembrance of former things; neither shall there be any remembrance of things that are to come with those that shall come after*".

These verses back up the straight truth earlier stated that there is no man so essential before God that cannot be replaced if he misbehaves.

When you have an opportunity to work for God, grab it with all your being because there might not be a second chance to make it up.

Below are illustrations for readers to know, confirm, accept and believe that there is no indispensable man. The simple exercises you will undertake shortly are meant to serve as reminders to put you back on track whenever your mind starts conjuring thoughts that make you feel you are irreplaceable, or when you feel important and your ego is in bloom; when you think you are the most qualified man and your absence would leave a hole that cannot be filled. Just follow the simple instructions and see to what extent it goes in making you humble.

Exercise 1

Get a bucket of full of water. Dip your hand into it up to your elbow, then withdraw the hand. What do you see? Withholding bubbling in the middle of the water. No matter how long it takes the water to attain a serene surface – a split second. That is the length of time it takes for God to strip a man of misused glory. God desires that we make good use of His gifts.

Exercise 2

Stand on a sandy surface. Draw a shape on the sand with your finger or a stick. Then wipe it. Can you still see the drawn shape? No! Unused gift or glory slips off within a blink of the eye.

Replacement or Substitution is possible

Being replaced or substituted by a stone does not necessarily mean a gravel would rise and take ones place but it could also mean so because nothing is impossible with God. It is an idiomatic expression that explains how God can raise a man who is seemingly unfit to take the place of the one who is generally thought the best. A stone is simply something of little or no value and or importance. A slave might take the place of a master. So also can a horse rider become bare-footed.

Going through the scriptures, we see stories of how God raised some people and brought down other. Your availability and preparedness will go a long way in determining what will happen to you.

After God had changed Hannah's story, from being a barren woman to a fruitful mother of children, she sang a song which reiterates the scriptures below.

1 Samuel 2:6-8, *"The LORD kills and makes alive; He brings down to the grave and*

brings up. The LORD makes poor and makes rich; He brings low and lifts up He raises the poor from the dust And lifts the beggar from the ash heap, To set them among princes And make them inherit the throne of glory" (NKJV)

The first can become the last and vice versa. A prison and a palace may have the same structural design but the residents of the two are at par. When prisoners are made to live in a palace, it ceases to be a palace and becomes a prison. So also, the status of a prison changes when the king and a queen move into it. A nonentity becomes a man of substance when he submits himself for the work of God and the glory of God locates him while the reverse is the case when glory departs from a man.

Joseph was a stone. He was of no importance apart from being a son. His added value of being the younger son was despised by his elder brothers but the Lord saw a reason for him to be raised and he also made himself available. He rose from being a jailed slave to the position of a Governor. Genesis 41:39-40. Another good example is David, a shepherd boy. He made himself available for the work of God and the Lord used him to bring down the hard-to-defeat Goliath. How about Jephthah the Gileadite in Judges 11:1-33? The nation of Israel was under a siege and needed a deliverer. Jephthah was the son of a harlot and had been exiled by his brethren. In spite of his low background, God's glory was upon him, so much so that the elders of his town sought him out, begged him to be their Captain. He led them to war and God gave him victory.

Are you in position of authority today? Do you misuse the position and the seat of power? Check yourself and assess if what you are doing brings glory to God. If not, repent or get ready to hand over to a stone. That stone could be your secretary or receptionist. Lazarus was of no better importance than bringing fleets of flies and spreading offensive smell yet the glory of God was revealed through him in heaven and the rich man was stripped of his glory and became a candidate of hell. When a man is replaced, he is either completely out or is present as a dummy.

A man who is replaced by a stone has lost his glory. Matthew 3:8-9 says, *"Bring forth therefore fruits meet for repentance: And think not to say within yourselves, We have Abraham to our father: for I say unto you that God is able of these stones to raise up children unto Abraham"* John the Baptist was addressing the Pharisees and the Sadducees who had come to his baptism. It was not enough to just come for baptism, they must bring forth fruits meet for repentance. It is not enough to be saved; the fruits in your life must show it. Your life must advertise the glory of God. These two verses enjoin followers of Christ (Christians) to do things that will show they have turned away from their sins. God is able to raise rocks and make descendants for Abraham; i.e. God can replace sons with stones if they refuse to act like sons.

God has made everybody uniquely. The purposes for which we were created may differ but all is aimed at returning glory to God and have his beauty revealed through us. A man who does not use his God-given potentials appropriately will be replaced. The potential of a man will not yield results if he does not show any form of readiness and zeal in doing the will of God.

Why God Will Not Use You

Many Christians today are not as successful as they ought to be. They are not being used by God in manifesting His glory because they have chosen not to be used. This is as a result of not learning the secrets of God's success; or not putting it into good practice. There are many of reasons why God would rather raise stones to replace men. Many or most certainly, all of those who are replaced or will be replaced have some issues which the Lord considers ungodly or not Christ like. They are sometimes subtle not easily noticeable in some cases but a major turn off for God.

1. **Pride**- An arrogant person will never be used of God because he will ascribe the result of his labour and effort to his ability. Such a person is a cheat who attempts to share God's glory with him. He will most definitely be replaced by a humble person.

2. **Disobedience**- A person who refuses to follow and live by the instructions of God will be discarded to make way for the obedient.

Other vices that will not allow a Christian to be used to reveal the glory of God are greed, selfishness, hatred, temperance, unfaithfulness, selfishness, blasphemy, gluttony, gossip and many others. Judas was a disciple of Jesus Christ. He had unfettered access to the most relevant person of his time. What a privilege! What honor! But he lost the glory to greed and his discipleship to Jesus was taken at no cost. Peter who was also a disciple mismanaged the beauty of God and lost his to fear. His denial of Jesus depicts unfaithfulness. Thank God he sought restoration and got it.

How Can I Make God Use Me?

Without reservation, this is one big question that troubles many Christians. Before I explain how you can make God use you, I will like to say that you need to first ask yourself this honest question, which is, Can God use me?"

Many people who live in sin and with little faith find it difficult to say 'Yes' or 'No' to the question. There is just one simple and straight answer to it and it is 'YES'. God would not have created you if He would not use you. He made you so that His glory can be revealed though your existence. Many Christians today have traded their rights as children of God for slavery to sin and that is why they have been forced to believe the lie of the devil that they cannot be used by God. It is never too late to turn to God and be used as long as one is still alive

God can use you if you are ready to be used. A good example is the thief on the right side of Jesus on the cross. He was condemned but he remembered that all things are possible with God. He believed that Jesus could help him even at that time. He took a desperate decision, a very great stride to escape eternal hell fire and he was happy for it. A little delay might have been too late for him but heaven smiled on him. Jesus accepted him and eternal life was granted him

Back to the subject of discussion; how can I make God use me?

1. Trust in God - Let God know that He is indeed all you have got in heaven and on earth. Give yourself to him wholeheartedly. That is the kind of person God wants. Someone who will go all out to trust for him. Jeremiah 17:5 says, *"Thus saith the Lord; Cursed be the man that trusteth in man, and maketh flesh his arm, and whose heart departeth from the LORD"*. Verse 7, *"Blessed is the man that trusteth in the LORD and whose hope the LORD is"*. Verse 13, *"O LORD, the hope of Israel, all that forsake thee shall be ashamed, and they that depart from me shall be written in the earth, because they have forsaken the LORD, the fountain of living waters"*.

2. Put God's kingdom first - It is recorded in Matthew 6:25, *"Therefore I say unto you, Take no thought for your life, what ye shall eat, or what ye shall drink, nor yet for your body, what ye shall put on. Is not life more than meat, and the body than raiment? Behold the fowls of the air: for they sow not, neither do they reap, nor gather into barns; yet your heavenly Father feedeth them. Are ye not much better than they? Which of you by taking thought can add one cubit unto his stature? And why take ye thought for raiment? Consider the lilies of the field, how they grow; they toil not, neither do they spin: And yet I say unto you, That even Solomon in all his glory was not arrayed like one of these".* Verse 31, *"Therefore take no thought, saying, what we shall eat? Or, What shall we drink? Or Wherewithal shall we be clothed?"* Verse 33, *"But seek ye first the kingdom of*

God, and his righteousness; and all these things shall be added unto you". The above verses explain what God can do with us and in us. If his glory could be revealed through the grass of the field and birds of the air which are less important than us; then He can do just more if we trust in Him and put his kingdom first thus allowing Him to use us as He desires. When we do so, we accept that he is the porter and we are the clay. He molds us in the shape He wants and the glory is returned to Him.

3. Obedience - A Christian who obeys the commands of God and walks in His light has peace. Such person is glory bound. He will be used and be used to replace weaker vessels who have not submitted themselves for use. Mark 1:17, *'And Jesus said unto them, come ye after me and I will make you to become fishers of men"*. Jesus, in that verse is not commanding everybody, he is only talking to those who are ready to obey him and be used as fishers of men.

4. Ask God for what you need- Matthew 7:8, *"For every one that asketh receiveth; and he that seeketh findeth; and to him that knocketh it shall be opened"*. A Christian must learn to present his desires before God who promise in Matthew 7:7 that we should *"Ask and it shall be given; seek, and ye shall find; knock and it shall be opened unto you:"* Whoever asks in faith and in truth that he be used receives answer to his cries. God is the answer to all questions, so we should ask until our joy is full.

4. Have faith rather than hope - Hope is quiet, passive and waits for time and turn. Faith is daring: it is expressive and explosives, loud and active. Faith calls forth what be not as though they were. If a man asks in faith that he be used, it will be unto him according to his faith. Faith is a way of challenging God to answer our prayers. It is also a means of declaring our desire to be used for God's glory.

Chapter Seven: Glory In Heaven

Have you ever pondered on the brevity of life? Truly, we are here today and gone tomorrow. James 4:14 says, *"Whereas you do not know what will happen tomorrow. For what is your life? It is even a vapor that appears for a little time and then vanishes away"* (NKJV). A man's life is described in the scripture in various ways. In Psalm 39:5, it is described as *"...an handbreadth... a vapor"*. Psalm 103:15 refers to as *"...grass: as a flower of the field"*. Apostle James in 1:11 calls it, *"grass that withereth and a flower that falleth"* (Paraphrased). God's servant, Job, in chapter 14:2 calls it *"a flower and is cut down and a shadow that continueth not"* (Paraphrased). Psalm 39:6 reiterates that it is like *"a shadow"*.

There is absolutely nothing in life that is certain. Riches may be lost in a day (Ecclesiastes. 5:14). A healthy man may be stricken with sickness the next minute (Job 2:7), Friends or close relatives may die (2 Samuel 19:4) so, why should you invest your life in that which is transient and will pass away. According to the word of God in Psalm 49:12 and Psalm 49:17-18, a man will not endure and when he dies, he will not take anything away. Is it then worth gambling away eternity for that which is temporary, uncertain and passing away? It is obvious as stated in the previous chapter that it is only while living that, a man can give glory to God or live for his glory as there is no glory in the grave. There will be glory in heaven only for those who glorified God while they were on earth.

Heaven is a place of unspeakable glory where the elect will live with one another in the immediate presence of God and the lamb. It is where they will behold him in all his glory face to face. It is a place where the curse of sin and all its effects for only the with Christ. Jesus says in Matthew 25:34," *Then the king will say to those on His right hand,' come, you blessed of My Father, inherit the kingdom prepared for you from the foundation of the world:*" (NKJV). It is a kingdom where Christ the Blessed One is king and the saints are "*...kings and priests to His God and Father...*"Revelation 1:6 (NKJV) and proclaimed by Peter as"... *a chosen generation, a royal priesthood, a holy nation, His own special people...* 1 Peter 2:9(NKJV).

The Blessedness of Heaven

I will like us to consider the blessedness of heaven from three perspectives.

a. The first one is that those who enter into glory to live with God in heaven shall be free from sin itself. Sin is the reason we experience pain, sorrow, sickness and even death. The true child of God longs to be where he will sin no more. Sin is the greatest enemy of those who love holiness. It makes war upon one as the flesh lusts against the Spirit and the Spirit against the flesh. In heaven we shall be free from sin.

b. The second blessing of heaven is that we shall be free from the causes of sin which are the sinful nature, the temptations of the devil and the lure of the world. The sinful nature is the source of the sins we commit according to James 1:14-15, which when fully grown leads to death. If you are a true believer, you will be free from the temptations in heaven. In this world, the devil is walking about, as a roaring lion, seeking whom he may devour (1 Peter 5:8) but in heaven, he will not be there as he would have been thrown into the bottomless pit. In heaven, men shall be free from the lusts of the world as described in 1 John 2:16. The lust of the flesh, the lust of the eyes and the pride of life are of the world and will pass away with it. In heaven the ungodly influences working with the corrupt nature would have been overcome through the blood of Jesus Christ.

c. The primary consequence of sin is eternal punishment in hell but for as many as will reign with Christ in heaven, they will be free from the consequences of sin. 1 Thessalonians 1:10 says, "And to wait for his Son from heaven, whom he raised from the dead, even Jesus, which delivered us from the wrath to come."

I think the only time we can fully understand this glory is when we get to heaven. We all must aspire to make it.

Benefits of Making Heaven

There are many benefits of making heaven. More of these benefits will be unraveled when we get Home but some are worth mentioning here.

A. The saints in heaven shall see God in all His majesty-We shall behold the infinite glory of the Almighty God in as great a capacity as they we are capable of. Matthew 5:8 says, "Blessed are the pure in heart, for they shall see God". God the Father will not directly manifest Himself because we are told in the scriptures that God is Invisible. I Timothy 1:17 says, *"Now unto the King eternal, immortal, invisible, the only wise God, be honour and glory for ever and ever. Amen"*

It is said of Christ in the scriptures "Who is the image of the Invisible God, the firstborn of every creature:" (Colossians 1:15). Not only will we see Christ face to face, but we will walk with Him and talk with Him. Jesus told his disciples while they were still clothed in their sinful nature, in John 15:15 that, *"No longer do I call you servants, for a servant does not know what his master is doing, but I have called you friends, for all things that I heard from My Father I have made known to you."* (NKJV). If Christ could say this to his disciples, don't you think he will admit them nearer him in heaven when they have been fully purged of all stain? Certainly, he will. The scriptures speak of God living with and among His people in a glorious term in Revelation 21:3 *"...the tabernacle of God is with men, and he will dwell with them, and they shall be His people, and God Himself will be with them and be their God* (NKJV) In Revelation 22:4, the Bible says, *"They shall see His face, and His name shall be on their foreheads"* (NKJV)

B. Those who are admitted to heaven shall enjoy the perfection of grace- *"For we know in part, and we prophesy in part. But when that which is perfect come, then that which is in part shall be done away"* (1 Corinthians 13: 9 -10)

Now, our knowledge of divine things are shallow and distinct but in heaven, we shall understand the Excellency of Christ to a full degree. Also, the grace of holiness shall be perfected in all who are received into glory."...*We know that, when he shall appear, we shall be like Him; for we shall see him as he is*" (1 John 3:2). Holiness is the transcendent beauty of God and the angels. In heaven, holiness will be perfected in the believer.

Those who are in heaven shall experience the fullness of joy. "...In thy presence is fullness of joy, at thy right hand there are pleasures for evermore" (Psalm 16:11). The fullness of joy can be described as the bountiful love of God which is as the water of an ocean. Seeing God, who loved us even before we knew Him and knowing that we are His beloved, will cause a jubilation of Spirit. It will create unspeakable raptures of joy in the saints.

How then are the saints in glory rewarded?

Apostle Paul's second letter to the Corinthians chapters 3:8 and 5:10 reveal that there will be different degrees of glory in heaven. *"For we must all appear before the judgment seat of Christ; that every one may receive the things done in his body, according to that he hath done, whether good or bad.* Each will receive his own reward according to his own labour." The scripture speaks of the one who receives "a prophet's reward" (Matthew 10:41), which distinguishes it from the ordinary one. In Daniel 12:3, the Bible says, "And they that be wise shall shine as the brightness of the firmament; and they that turn many to righteousness as the stars forever and ever. Paul also compares the sun, moon and stars in glory. So also is the resurrection of the dead". (1 Corinthians 15:41-42). Paul is saying that just as one star shines more brightly than another, so also, one saint shall shine with more heavenly glory. Based on how they had lived and what they had done for Christ, while on earth. This is alluded to in the parable of the talents, where one man is given authority over ten cities and another over five (Luke 19:12-19).

Who is qualified for heaven's glory?

"And an highway shall be there, and a way, and it shall be called The way of holiness; the unclean shall not pass over it; but it shall be for those: the wayfaring men, though fools, shall not err therein" (Isaiah 35:8) Heaven cannot be attained by the lazy and the slothful, or the unclean and the profane. Not even by those who are unholy church attendees. The way to heaven is indeed "a highway of holiness" and it is for "him who walks that

way" that is, it is for the one who lives a holy life. In Matthew 5:8, Christ says; *"Blessed are the pure in heart: for they shall see God"*. Heaven is for the pure in heart and lovers of God.

Finally, I will like you to consider your body and your soul. Matthew 16:26 says *"For what is a man profited, if he shall gain the whole world, and lose his own soul? or what shall a man give in exchange for his soul?"* Your soul is more valuable than your body. The body will die and rot in the grave but the soul will live forever. So then, compare and contrast the time you spend in taking care of your body and the time you invest in eternal life for your soul. Examine yourself thoroughly and do the needful.

Do you indulge sin? Do you hate all sin as sin? Who or what dominates your thoughts and desire? Is it Jesus or the world? Do you love Jesus for who He is or just for what He can do for you? Do you like holiness and obedience to the word of God or is it burdensome to you? Do you really love God or do you just fear His stand on judgment? Do not just read these questions. Many who profess to be Christianity today are simply religious and not regenerated

Do you know that those who run in a race all run, but only one receives the prize? Run in such a way that you may win...'that the GLORY of the Lord may appear unto you' (Lev.9:6b) and that ye might....receive a crown of that fadeth not away'... (1Peter 5:4b).

Conclusion

Ponder on this song by Chicago Mass Choir:

Chorus

I pray we'll all be ready.

I pray we'll all be ready.

I pray we'll all be ready for his return.

I pray that we'll get our business straight.

So we can all meet at the gate.

I pray we'll all be ready for His return.

Verse 1

Two men walking by the road

One of them had a heart pure as gold.

The sky was split and the pure in heart

raptured away.

But one of the other one left behind who did not purge his heart in time

Cried to the Lord but for him it is too late.

I pray that we'll all be ready.

Verse 2

Man and wife in their bed

One of them by the Spirit lead

The rapture came and took that one above.

The other one rose on the next day to find their loved one raptured away

Oh what a way to lose the one you love.

I pray we'll all be ready.

Oh, oh, I pray

I pray that we'll all be ready

I pray that we'll all be ready

For His return

I pray that we'll give our hearts a search

So that we won't be playing church

I pray we'll all be ready for His return

Verse 3

Momma and children in the mall

Their momma heard the Master's call

She was swept into the sky by and by

It's hard to rely on your momma's prayer

When your momma is no longer there

Learn how to pray, learn how to pray

While you still have time.

Chorus

I pray we'll all be ready

I pray we'll all be ready

I pray we'll all be ready for his return.

I pray that we'll get our business straight.

So we can all meet at the gate.

I pray we'll all be ready for His return

Other Books by the Same Author

1. Talk Right: An Effective Prayer Companion

2. See Right: Winning By Sight

3. Right Success: Secrets To Ultimate Breakthroughs

4. Right Hand: The Mystery Of Divine Hand

About the Author

Wale Oyeniyi is a man of many parts. He is a Teacher, an Author, a Speaker, a Preacher, an Educationist, a Philanthropist and an Entrepreneur.

An Alumnus of Obafemi Awolowo University (OAU), The Redeemed Christian Church of God Bible College and Haggai Institute, USA. He has attended several leadership courses at home and abroad

He is a friend and mentor to many people around the world. He is an adherent proponent of leadership by example. He is much sought after as a speaker in churches, seminars and conferences

He is the President of Betterlife© International, an NGO that amongst other things specialize in organizing counseling, educating Young Adults, Youths and leaders of businesses and ministers of the Gospel.

He is happily married and resides with his family in Lagos.

www.ingramcontent.com/pod-product-compliance
Lightning Source LLC
Chambersburg PA
CBHW051448250726
48655CB00001B/309